Recollections of Lincoln

[Reprinted from the BIBLIOTHECA SACRA,
October, 1908, pp 636-656.]

ARTICLE III.

RECOLLECTIONS OF LINCOLN

BY HONORABLE J. O. CUNNINGHAM, URBANA, ILLINOIS.

> "His was no lofty mountain-peak of mind,
> Thrusting to thin air o'er cloudy bars,
> A sea-mark now, now lost in vapors blind;
> Broad prairie rather, genial, level-lined,
> Fruitful and friendly for all human kind,
> Yet also nigh to heaven and loved of loftiest stars,
>
> .   .   .   .
>
> For many a year and many an age
> While History on her ample page
>   The virtues shall enroll
>   Of that paternal soul!"—RICHARD HENRY STODDARD.

No name in American history evokes greater interest and enthusiasm, not only among Americans, but also among the people of all civilized lands, than does that of the name of our first martyred president.

Great events and sad events in our national history transpiring since he ceased to live and act, have failed to dim the public interest in him. More than this, his name has become permanently etched upon the World's scroll of fame as a benefactor of races and as an exponent of true nobility of character. Notoriety has given to others an evanescent fame which fades with half a generation, but it is a lofty character and personality alone which wins for one the position occupied by him in history!

The reasons underlying and making possible this condition are not solely due to his public career as President of a mighty nation and the Emancipator of a race from human chatteldom, but rather or quite materially to reasons connected with his personality as a man and member of society before his advancement to the presidential chair This period of his life distinguishes him and his relations to history over the great majority of men who have succeeded in raising themselves above the common herd of humanity.

It was during this period of his life, his unofficial and professional life, that the writer, from political and professional associations, was given opportunities for a somewhat close acquaintance with and study of the man.

On the fourteenth day of February, 1809, there was born to Thomas Lincoln and his wife, Nancy Hanks Lincoln, in their primitive, windowless, cabin home, in what was then Hardin County, Kentucky, the child Abraham: so called for his paternal grandfather, whose tragic death at the hands of a band of marauding Indians a few years prior had helped to paint the " dark and bloody " soil of that State.

It was to no life of luxury and ease that this child of the forest was born! Fortunately for him and for his country, " poor white " parentage did not entail poverty in mental and moral qualities; nor does a low financial condition of parentage necessarily destine the subject to a lowly life American history is rich in instances wherein the highest offices have been filled by the offspring of the class known in the South as " poor white trash," who have transmitted, unimpaired, mental qualities inherent in the Scotch and British ancestry which originally peopled the mountains and frontiers of that section.

Lincoln was born to orphanage—for, at an early age, he lost his mother by an untimely death: to a life of toil: to a heritage of debt: to a youth of struggle for existence. In his boyhood, no partial friend made the acquisition of knowledge easy to

him and paved the way to collegiate honors; no ample library
at his home or town afforded him the means for the acquisition
of such knowledge nor for mental recreation, no graded school
received him at the age of six and matriculated him in college
at sixteen. His childhood, that usual period of poetry, was
devoid of every ease, and he was early in life inured to toil and
privation. His school of science was only the open book of
Nature as revealed in the woods and hills of Kentucky and
Indiana. His only helps in getting on in the world were his
brawny hands and his stout heart, spurred on by an American
boy's ambition. He wore the homespun clothing of flax and
wool wrought by the loving and nimble fingers of his mother,
and he early exchanged the ease of infancy for the labors of
the fields and the woods. His hours of recreation were taken
from those of repose, and his hands were calloused by the use
of the axe and the plow.

While stately mansions in the surroundings of cultured re-
finement furnished the homes of such of his predecessors in
the presidency as the Adamses, Madison, Monroe, and Van
Buren, the rude forest cabin was the home of Lincoln during
his childhood, and the feeble firelight his evening cheer. Even
when professional success had made life for him easier, it
brought with it none of the habits and surroundings of luxury.

His story, from his cabin home in Kentucky to abundant
professional success in Illinois and finally to the presidential
mansion, was the story of Garfield and of McKinley and of
many another youth who, if not reaching presidential honors
and worldly renown, has by well-directed efforts earned fame
in other directions, and has taught other aspiring youths the
possibilities within the reach of the helpless but ambitious poor
who are so fortunate as to be born under our liberal institu-
tions.

Nature made Lincoln a nobleman and a ruler of men: a humble and obscure birth and the adverse surroundings of his childhood and early manhood failed to stamp out the impress!

The numerous and well-written histories of Mr. Lincoln tell the story of his life from the cabin to the White House from a public standpoint; but they only scantily tell of his life upon the eighth Judicial Circuit of Illinois, where, from the year 1836 to 1860, at the first as a briefless barrister, he wooed success at the bar and in politics, at the beginning with but a poor equipment of legal learning, and later on professional success as an able and conscientious lawyer. Here he was matured, and that character which so makes for him among men was strengthened. Here the writer first met him, and in this capacity, and as a campaigner in the political contests occurring there once in two years, best knew him.

The reader, unacquainted with the unavoidable conditions surrounding the administration of justice in all newly and sparsely settled countries, will need be told that to reach the present condition of dignity and propriety always looked for and found in our courts of justice in the states of the Middle West, a long stride has been made and primitive conditions have been overcome.

When Jacob Burnett traveled a circuit extending from the Ohio River to Lake Erie, and George Tod held all the Common Pleas courts in Northern Ohio, each traveling on horseback, with perhaps a retinue of lawyers in his train, from county to county, spending nights in the shelter of the woods, or better, if so fortunate, in some friendly cabin along the route, and dispensed justice in some log court-house from improvised " benches," a day or so at each county, a very different condition prevailed from that now seen in the same territories, where, from many elegant court-houses and with a uniform formality, the same laws are enforced by many judges for the benefit of a dense and wealthy population.

Similar conditions prevailed in Central Illinois during a large part of the time while Lincoln was upon the circuit. Judges Samuel H. Treat and David Davis, his successor, for many years held the *nisi prius* courts in the fourteen counties of the eighth Judicial Circuit, which territory extended from the Illinois River on the west to the Indiana line on the east, and included Springfield, the home of Lincoln.

These judges, like Judges Burnett and Tod in Ohio, in turn traveled their circuit on horseback or in rude wagons, with the usual retinue of lawyers following, of whom, and at least semi-annually, Lincoln was one for many years up to 1860. Urbana, the residence of the writer during many of these years, was the seat of justice for Champaign County, and there Mr. Lincoln, from his frequent visits as a lawyer, was well known to all, and his presence upon the streets was a familiar one. This was the common lot of all lawyers who as early as the period of which this is written wooed success in the profession, except in the counties more densely inhabited. Hard fare, small fees, and little of reputation among a limited clientage were in most cases the first-fruits of this life.

This long-continued association between the two chief characters above alluded to—Judge Davis and Mr. Lincoln—continued for half a lifetime as lawyers traveling the circuit together, or as judge and practising lawyer when one had been elevated to the bench, and begat, as was natural where mutual confidence exists as in that case, a most intimate and close friendship between them, which continued unabated to the last.[1]

[1] Singularly enough, it was Judge Davis, the bosom friend and companion of the War President, whom he, at the first opportunity

This life upon the circuit as a lawyer, varied by his participation in the biennial political contests, upon which Mr. Lincoln entered when admitted to the bar in 1836, brought him constantly into close contact with the common people as suitors, witnesses, jurors, as well as with the cabin dwellers along the traveled roads and traces leading from county-seat to county-seat. They were largely of the same classes of people among whom he had been born and with whom he had dwelt in Indiana and at New Salem. These associations tended to continue in him a love for plain language, plain people, and plain living, including a homely style of expressing himself in conversation, upon the rostrum, before juries, and in putting his thoughts upon paper, now so much admired by even critics, who have made a study of his speeches and papers. Under the changed conditions of his later life, he never seemed to seek to throw off those early habits of living, thinking, and speaking, further than to remedy the defects in pronunciation and grammar; for his language, as it is remembered and as it has been preserved to us in his speeches, is as correct in diction as it is homely in style, and free from pedantry and excessive use of words.

In court Mr. Lincoln was always genial and courteous, never quarreling with either the court or with his brother lawyers. His arguments to juries were plain talks, becoming emphatic as the occasion required. The writer served upon a jury after he had attained the high office, elevated to the Supreme Federal bench, who, after the death of the President, when all heads and hearts were well cooled, upon the consideration of the Milligan case, imprisoned by a military court for alleged disloyalty, announced the unanimous opinion of that high court in condemnation of the assumption of the power by the President and military courts to imprison Northern men for alleged disloyalty, where the ordinary courts of the country were unimpeded in the exercise of an unquestioned jurisdiction for the punishment of such offenders.

but once in his life, and then Lincoln was the attorney for one of the parties, and his methods were carefully observed and noted. One telling peculiarity of his, in entering upon an argument of this kind, was to begin by conceding to his adversary every point in the case contended for by him which was not in his estimation material and vital, or which might safely be granted, thus at once disposing of irrelevant points and giving the impression of fairness to his opponent. This done, but no more, his manner changed; and, with the expression "But," he would very simply and plainly point out to his jury, who by this time he had well won to him, the real and vital points upon which the case must turn, and would apply the evidence in the case so as to show that the only conclusion possible for the jury must sustain his client's case. If the evidence failed to make this course of argument possible, and showed the right and law to be with his opponent, Lincoln was disarmed, for the art of dissimulation was to him unknown.

That he never took cases lacking merit, and in fact tried his client's case and rendered judgment before accepting it, discarding all cases not absolutely meritorious, as some writers have claimed, is a fiction of the imagination of these biographers. Like other lawyers, he desired the strong side of the case, but he recognized in all cases the right of a candid client or accused person to a fair trial, and to have his case honestly presented to the court and jury to the best advantage, with all the presumptions of the law in his favor. This is a course always possible and within the bounds of the most exacting propriety.

Some commentators upon the life and associations of Mr. Lincoln have with much minuteness, and as much error, left it to be understood that in his intercourse with his associates the lowest familiarity on the part of his companions was exercised and tolerated, in that he was constantly addressed and referred to in his presence by the name of "Abe." Nothing could be said upon this phase of his life which would be more erroneous. He was generally addressed by those approaching his age by the name of " Lincoln," only; while we of the younger men who were occasionally with him always addressed him as " Mr. Lincoln," with the proper deference. It is probable that with his more intimate friends of New Salem and Springfield, the familiar nickname may have been made use of, but what these pages profess to tell is of his life upon the circuit and upon the stump. It is certain that in the descriptions of his great debates with Judge Douglas, who had known him before then many years and intimately, no justification is found for the claim made in favor of this low familiarity on the part of his associates.

Some instances of the demeanor of Mr. Lincoln falling under the observation of the writer will well illustrate how naturally, and at all times and without seeming thought or effort, he met the people upon the same level upon which he and they had been bred, may not be out of point.

On the day preceding the now celebrated Bloomington Convention, held at Bloomington, on May 29, 1856, it having been the first state gathering of the elements which, when united, formed the Republican party of Illinois, Mr. Lincoln was in attendance upon the Circuit Court at Danville, in Eastern Illinois, but with the determination to attend this call and with an intense desire that the convention should not be a failure for the want of numbers The week previous he had attended the same Court at Urbana, Judge David Davis presiding at both. He had talked the matter of the coming convention with political friends in both counties, and on that day, with quite a following from both Vermilion and Champaign counties, mostly of young men and sympathizers, of whom the writer was one, was upon his way to Bloomington. His route led the company by the Wabash Railroad to Decatur, and thence, by the Illinois Central Railroad, to Bloomington. We arrived at Decatur about the middle of the afternoon, but too late for a train to our destination that day, making a stay there over night necessary. The afternoon and evening were to be disposed of in some way; and, as was his custom when leisure permitted, he said to our crowd, " Boys, let us go to the woods " This was assented to, and, led by him, we went down to the timber belt then skirting the Sangamon River, half a mile away. There we arrived, and were soon seated upon the body of a fallen tree, lying near the road in a thicket of brush. For some hours in the shade and suitably situated for recreation, we remained in conversation, mostly upon the topic uppermost in the minds of all, the coming convention and its results; but also listening to Lincoln's stories and quaint expressions. His manner with his young followers that long afternoon was as intimate and informal as if he had again met there the young men and boys of New Salem, and was again entertaining them with his drolleries. The occasion was one in which he exhibited what some one has called his " grand ungainliness." His interest in the coming convention and its outcome occupied most of his attention, and seemed to be upon his mind, but other and familiar topics were talked.

The next day at the convention, to which further reference is hereafter made, which proved one of great interest and was in fact an important epoch in the state history, he met the foremost men of the old Whig party, with whom he had in the past years always gone down to defeat, politically, as well as many prominent Democrats, who were in a state of revolt against Judge Douglas's leadership; also men of the former Anti-slavery party, a mass of men as yet disunited and in a measure discordant, except upon the one idea of opposition to the extension of slavery into the territories, made possible by the late legislation in Congress, for which they held Douglas responsible.

In this gathering, Lincoln, probably for the first time in his life, showed his great qualities of leadership. It was not the leadership of the mere politician, but that generalship which at once takes into consideration the end to be accomplished in the future, the material available, and the immediate and remote obstacles to be overcome. The odds and ends of the old parties not in sympathy with Douglas were at hand and available if fusion was possible In the way of a complete union were certain old issues of the old parties, now latent to a hopeful extent, and the intense horror of the conservative element of the epithet *abolitionist!* But Douglas had in a manner helped in this, for he had long since, and in every speech made by him, called them all *"Black Republicans,"* the sting of which had in two years partly worn off. The work of fusion was well accomplished by the contact of mind with mind, and the discovery of the fact that they were one upon the only issue which would divide parties at the coming national election, and an acceptable declaration of principles was agreed upon. A ticket drawn from all elements represented, headed by Colonel William H. Bissell for Governor, was put before the people. Mr. Lincoln himself was made head of the electoral ticket, and really led the party to a triumphant success so far as the state ticket was concerned, though Mr. Buchanan carried the electoral election. This was the first time in the history of the State of Illinois when a Governor was elected not of the party of Judge Douglas.

The contrast between the conduct of the Lincoln of May 28,

on the train *en route* tc Bloomington and upon the log in the
Sangamon woods, in company with his young partisan followers,—plebeian in demeanor, gay, story-telling, and common in
every respect,—and the Lincoln in his appearance and actions
before the convention, the moving spirit in a mass of unorgan-
ized but zealous men whom it was desirable to unite in a common purpose in behalf of a great movement of the nation for
humanity, was a revelation of his true character and power!
There, by his mastery of the situation and his moving elo-
quence, he made himself a state leader, as he became six years
thereafter a national leader! In the former attitude he was a
boy among boys, his equals there! In the latter he was a leader
of leaders among men in a great and untried contest, in which
he successfully mobilized discordant elements into a united
party and led the men forth harmonious and to conquest!

Here for the first time, it is claimed, Mr Lincoln exhibited
the qualities of leadership which during the great Rebellion he
proved himself to possess in so eminent a degree. Those only
who know the wide breach which before 1856 separated the
Whigs and Democrats of Illinois from the Anti-slavery party,
which had no existence in that State save in the northern counties, and were universally known by the offensive epithet of
"*abolitionists,*" can understand the real difficulties of the task
undertaken and accomplished at Bloomington That O H.
Browning, John M. Palmer, John Wentworth, and Archibald
Williams, representative men of the old parties, should affiliate
and co-labor in a political campaign with Owen Lovejoy, President Blanchard, and Ichabod Codding, upon a well-defined
platform of principles, based upon opposition to the spread of
slavery in the territories, leaving out of sight the moral aspects
of that institution where it had legal existence, as well as the
debatable questions in economics which before then had

always divided the Whig and Democratic parties, was the
anomaly and wonder of the day! It is no less so at this time,
with those who survive and understand the then situation! The
men who constituted that convention having mostly passed
away, it is now recognized that to the initiative genius and
generalship of Lincoln was it all due. The conclusion is the
correct one.

In October, 1858, and during the contest between himself
and Judge Douglas, Mr. Lincoln had an appointment to speak
at the Fair Ground at Urbana. He came to the grounds at the
head of an immense delegation of citizens, in wagons and upon
horseback, which had met him at the railroad station. His
friends among the ladies in charge of the tables where the inev-
itable barbecue of all political gatherings of that day was to
be served to the people at the noon hour, had prepared for him
and for his immediate attendants a place at the head of the
tables, where the best of the feast had been placed for his use.
He was met at the gate and escorted to the place prepared for
him at the head of the tables, and was seated and engaged in
disposing of his dinner, when his eye fell upon an old woman
standing not far away and looking intently at him. He
at once, recognizing the woman, asked her, "Why, Gran-
ny," a name by which he and others were in the habit of
calling her, "have you no place to eat your dinner?" He had
known her as a waiter and helper about the hotel where he had
been in the habit of stopping The woman answered him that
she did not want dinner, "Just wanted to see you, Mr. Lincoln." He would not have it so, but said, "You must have a
place, here, come and take my place." This the old lady per-
sistently refused, until he arose and made her take his seat at
the table while he, with his turkey leg, and bread and butter,
sat down upon the ground at the foot of a near-by tree, and

there finished his luncheon. This done, he took his place in the speakers' stand before a large audience, where Judge Douglas had the day before spoken, and for an hour and a half in his trenchant and plain manner, which all could understand, exposed the fallacies of "Squatter Sovereignty," under the Dred Scott decision.

Some censorious critic may draw satisfaction in saying that the event of giving his seat to this humble woman was a piece of "acting," for effect. Not so. In his feelings towards his fellow-creatures, Lincoln knew no such thing as caste. His chivalrous feelings towards woman did the rest!

Some years since, as the writer was passing the residence of a neighbor, an elderly lady of Urbana, an old resident there, who was an acquaintance of Mr. Lincoln, one known to him as an emigrant from one of the Southern States, he found her in the garden upon her knees, gathering herbs for a mess of "greens." A familiar salutation as to her occupation caused her to look up from under her sun-bonnet with the exclamation, "I was just thinking of Lincoln Once he came along when I was gathering greens in the spring, back in the fifties, as I am now, and said to me, ' That's right, Mrs. K., get plenty of greens, and I will come and take dinner with you.' " She further said that Mr. Lincoln, at the noon hour, did come and take dinner with her family, and said she, "And you ought to have seen him eat the greens and bacon!"

These incidents are narrated to illustrate the habitual simplicity of the thoughts and character of the man. He never sought to cast behind him, as something to be discarded and forgotten with its associations, that life to which he was born and reared. It and his surroundings in his childhood and young manhood, as he well knew, had for him no lessons in jurisprudence or statecraft, and served no purpose, other than to minister to his democratic and agrarian instincts and tastes.

As a lawyer in the Supreme Court and upon the circuit, he associated with such brilliant minds as Judges Treat and Davis, Leonard Swett, Usher F. Linder, O. B. Ficklin, E. D. Baker, O L. Davis, and William D. Somers, some of whom reached high positions in political and professional life, all of whom were deep students of legal and classical literature, which encouraged in him the cultivation of the logical and measured style of language used by him in conversation, in his addresses, and in his published papers His style of expression the ablest critics have deferred to as faultless.

As above briefly pictured, with the exception of three terms as a member of the legislative body of Illinois and one term as a member of the lower house of Congress, Mr. Lincoln spent his life up to and until the year 1854, when he had attained the age of forty-five.   This date, so pivotal in the life of the nation, was in his life no less important.   At this time Senator Douglas, an early and successful opponent, by his discovery of the misfit doctrine of " Squatter Sovereignty," furnished the opportunity for the passing of Lincoln from a mediocre life to the eminence which the world recognizes

The logical effect of the Kansas-Nebraska bill, which that year became a law, was not only to organize unoccupied territory into inchoate states of the Federal family, but to pave the way for the unannounced " Dred Scott " decision of the Supreme Court.   In appearance and according to the explanation of Douglas, it was a kind of local option, as applied to human slavery.   It in effect said, Let each territory and state determine for itself whether or not it will enslave and make chattels of one part of its inhabitants, who must spend their lives and devote their offspring for the benefit of the dominating class It had in its favor a corruption of the principle uppermost in the American mind, that all power is inherent in the people, and that a majority of that people must control; but it fatally ignored the rights of the minority, and failed to limit the power of the majority within the bounds of human freedom and equal rights. Whenever local option attempts to set up a system which goes beyond the limits of morality, and fosters a condition of immorality; or when it interferes with the right of every man to "eat the bread his own hands have earned," it becomes subversive of the ends of human government This in effect the new discovery did. The wrong could be read between the lines of that law, and so was read by Lincoln while "on the circuit." His incisive intellect saw the vulnerable point in the coat of mail with which Douglas had clothed himself, and, like Goliath of old, had walked forth upon the plains of Illinois, and with words of defiance challenged the hosts of abolitionism to battle. Lincoln was the unknown David of that day. To the challenge of the "Little Giant," "Choose you a man for you, and let him come down to me," he came forth, and, laying aside the armor and political toggery of Whiggery with which his old associates would have encumbered him, he "chose him five smooth stones out of the brook,"—the simple life, human rights, truth, consistency, and plain talk,—and, going forth with the sling of his unclouded intellect, accepted the challenge of the boastful giant.

The Philistine chieftain "disdained" the champion of the army of right. No less than this did Judge Douglas to Lincoln, when in effect he said to him, "Am I a dog, that thou comest to me with staves?" When Douglas at Galesburg, an anti-slavery town, threatened, when he had led Lincoln down into Egypt, to warp him to destruction, he, no less than the Philistine, in effect said to his humble adversary, "Come to me, and I will give thy flesh unto the fowls of the air, and to the beasts of the field!"

The scriptural parallel may be further invoked, for Lincoln, in reply to Douglas's boastful demeanor, in effect said, " Thou comest to me with a sword and with a spear, and with a shield : but I come to thee in the name of the Lord of hosts, the God of the armies of Israel, whom thou hast defied !"

The termination of both contests above referred to was similar ! Truth, though championed by humble agents, will always prevail !

Recurring to the date, 1854. Lincoln first attacked Douglas's new discovery in a speech at Springfield, delivered on October 3, the next day after one by Douglas at the state house. This was followed by another at Peoria on October 16, and on October 24 at Urbana. To the latter the writer for the first time listened to a political address from Mr. Lincoln. This speech was in fact the third in which he had purposely attacked the aggressiveness of slavery, and indirectly at least the institution itself. The writer, then fresh from the influences and radicalism of a childhood training in Northern Ohio, and Oberlin, was impatient at the reserve with which the speaker handled the slavery question, he scarcely alluding to its moral phases , but, basing his objections to the then late legislation in Congress, upon the fact that in the territory affected by it slavery had once and for a consideration been excluded and it solemnly dedicated to freedom, he ignored all moral questions. He there exhibited none of the freedom of criticism of the system and of its influence upon the nation which characterized his later utterances in 1856 and 1858. The reasons for this were afterwards obvious. He was then addressing, not an audience of Ohio radicals, but one, as he well knew, made up mostly of men who had never listened to an anti-slavery address, and who were alarmed at the name of *abolitionist,* being mostly immigrants from slaveholding states. Largely they were the old Whig friends and adherents of Lincoln, whom he was seeking to win as allies against this new, and by its plausibility misleading, doctrine. To have dealt with the slavery question then as he did four years thereafter, when engaged in the contest with his adversary, would have been at once to drive from him these old friends of his to the Douglas standard. He well knew the situation and its dangers at that period

From what has been learned of the actual sentiments of Mr. Lincoln as indicated by some of his earlier and unguarded expressions, at that time and for many years before then, his real convictions upon the moral phases of the slavery question underwent no changes from the episode in political affairs which called him forth in 1854 He long before then saw and appreciated the wrongs against humanity permitted by it, but was restrained from giving utterance to his convictions

At the Bloomington convention of May 29, 1856, above referred to, he spoke under the same guarded limitations as at Urbana, in 1854. The time had not yet come for the full utterance of his convictions. There too he had before him an aggregation of former Democrats and Whigs who as yet held but one sentiment in common, that of opposition to the legislation promoted by Senator Douglas, whom he hoped, by wise manipulation, to unite in an effective opposition. With them was also another element, the anti-slavery men from the northern counties, of the Lovejoy and Codding variety, willing and anxious for a coalition with the former, but whose radicalism was to the others as a red flag held before a wild bull! The Whigs and Democrats, bred to a dislike for each other, were united in a dislike for the anti-slavery men which amounted in some cases to abhorrence! Lincoln was the last speaker of the day, Whigs, Democrats and Free-soilers having in turn had their innings. The then anarchy prevailing in Kansas, the legitimate fruit of the legislation complained of, was most largely

the theme for all speakers who preceded him. Fresh news
that day received of the most exciting and aggravating character, together with the actual presence at the convention, as
speakers, of the expelled Governor Reeder and other exiles
from that territory, gave to all speakers a text from which to
enlarge, and the topic had well been worked over, all alike con-
demning the policy of the administration in its dealings with
the vexed question, the intensity in the case of each speaker
depending upon the fact of his former party affiliations. Conservative men only counseled abiding by law methods, while
those more radical even justified a resort to extreme measures,
in which Sharpe's rifles were recommended

After the settlement of the question of a platform and of
candidates, Mr. Lincoln, who had until then been busy in the
committees, was called to the platform, and was indeed needed
in order that the excitement, then at the fever heat, be allayed
With a coolness that contrasted with that of the convention,
he began his address with a mild but well-understood rebuke
of the counseled force of previous speakers, telling his audience to "Wait until November, and then to shoot paper bal-
lots at them." Having administered an effective sedative to
his audience, he entered upon a most logical and convincing
arraignment of Senator Douglas and the administration of Mr.
Buchanan for the condition approaching war between the sec-
tions then prevailing in Kansas, quite suggestive of an approaching national climax. He compared the then condition
of affairs in the country with that which preceded the legislation of 1854, and charged the unfortunate change, which then
threatened consequences so direful, to the ambitions of Douglas! Particularly did he deplore what the South even then
threatened, disunion of the States, and in the severest terms
denounced the growing sentiment looking to that condition of

national affairs which five years thereafter became effective !

His arguments left for his hearers no other conclusion than that a working union of all parties opposed to Douglas and his ticket, before then placed in the field, must be effected. In this speech no allusion was made which could alarm his conservative friends from the southern part of the State, while the other element from the north end were delighted and encouraged to find so able and logical an advocate against the aggressions of slavery

At that time the term " Republican," as a party designation, had been but little used in Illinois, and that by the free-soil element only. The convention had been called as an "Anti-Nebraska Convention", and by this designation only from an abundance of caution, did Lincoln allude to it in his speech He wisely knew that his conservative friends had gathered there, not purposely to commit themselves to whatever might be brought forth by the gathering, but rather with a mental reservation which would permit their support or opposition to its work, according as they might see it when completed, and that to alarm them might start a stampede which would result in complete defeat. Hence his caution and moderation.

As elsewhere indicated, the events and results of this memorable convention firmly fixed the position of Mr. Lincoln as the leader of the new party in Illinois. His ability, wisdom, and moderation well marked him as the man to lead the opposition to Senator Douglas, and this, from this time henceforth, he did, by unanimous approval

Douglas and Lincoln as competitors in the political field began their contests many years before this, when both were but beginners in the profession of the law in adjoining counties, and were likewise both members of the legislative body. Few of the state campaigns which took place between the years

1836 and 1860 but they contested upon the same territory for
personal and political success, besides contending together in
behalf of clients in the Supreme and Circuit courts   It was
no new experience with them when, in 1858, by the action of
their parties, they were made the champions for each upon the
only issue which at that day divided them.   Each knew the
other thoroughly, and both entered the contest with a full
knowledge of what he had to meet.   Douglas had the advantage in having at all times before 1860 met with success, except
in one contest, that for a seat in the Lower House of Congress,
for he became Attorney-General for the State at the age of
twenty-two; a judge of the Supreme Court at the age of
twenty-eight; a member of Congress at the age of thirty, a
United States Senator at the age of thirty-three, and a formid-
able candidate for the presidency at the age of thirty-nine.
Before that age he had a well-earned reputation as an able
politician in national affairs, while Mr Lincoln had, until 1860,
been with the losing party in his state, and had been a principal
actor in its many defeats.

These contests between the champions which began upon
and for so many years raged over the prairies of Illinois, and
which have given to the political and historical literature of the
country some of its brightest pages, ended, as every school-boy
knows, at the doors of the White House, with Lincoln as the
successful one at last, and with Douglas at death's door, for he
passed away within five months after taking part in the inaug-
uration of President Lincoln, having with his dying breath
spoken patriotic words of cheer and encouragement to his successful rival in his encounter with secession and rebellion,
which had been hastened perhaps by their contest in Illinois.

It is claimed above that to the personal peculiarities in the
character of Mr Lincoln, a love of justice, and a conscientious

adherence to truth, he owed his final success   All this he possessed in his earlier life, when he actively advocated the economic doctrines of the Whig party and when he always went down to defeat.   But when, in addition to this, his lips had been touched with the fires from humanity's altar, and he became the champion of human freedom, he triumphed, once for all, over his rival, and the world looked upon him with wonder and delight!

Lightning Source UK Ltd.
Milton Keynes UK
UKHW020600231119
354009UK00007B/198/P